The Model

MOLLY THOKWANA

Pharos Books

ISBN: 978-93-91384-31-9
eISBN: 978-93-91384-37-1

©Publishers

Publisher: Pharos Books (P) Ltd.
Plot No.-55, Main Mother Dairy Road
Pandav Nagar, East Delhi-110092
Phone: +14049995474
WhatsApp: +14049995474
E-mail: sales@pharosbooks.in
Website: www.pharosbooks.in
Edition: 2021

The Model
Molly Thokwana

Introduction

The Model is a book that gives a review and acts as a guideline on some of the most important aspects that can be of assistance to models. We, the authors of the book went through a process of general research which eventually led to evaluating models after having observed them. This research was undertaken for a period of three years, during which we held fashion shows, met models, interviewed them and got to know and learn more about their lifestyle.

The research has proved to us that models are quite unique brands. They are determined and influential beings and that grit propels them to want to do more in life. Apart from just being brands on their own, models can also act as representatives of a company, using their popularity to advertise it and its products. This book is designed to guide the models, educate them and challenge the status quo in the modelling industry. It's there to give knowledge and encourage models to view themselves as more than just "outside beauty bearers" but more as hosts of power and even intellect.

Preface

It's a journey that most want to take but unfortunately fail at. It is unfulfilled promises, malicious contracts and ignorance, all of which are the ingredients in the concoction that makes models quit before they even begin. It's that fear that breaks their spirits and causes them to lose hope.

It's about not knowing how to invest in one's talent, especially after a series of mishaps and regrets. It's giving it all that one has and still not getting the desired results. The motive behind this book is to try and give light were there seems to be no light, guide and direct models on what they should do and what to also avoid as they face the pressures of the harsh modelling industry.

Acknowledgements

We thank God for the completion of this book. Unbelievable amounts of gratefulness go out to our friends and motivators.

Special thanks go to the model social club, the boot camp models, African portfolio models and all the other people who took time to look at the book and offered advice on it.

A lot of gratitude also goes out to our respective parents and families, for their unending love, support and encouragement.

Contents

The Model

A model is an individual who acts as both a brand and a brand ambassador. They are a brand in the sense that they create a name for themselves by building a portfolio. That name then becomes a trademark which they use to attract job offers. On the other side of the two fold, they double as a brand envoy for the companies that require their services.

While modelling is a viable career path on its own, it is advisable that one considers it, as part time job. This conclusion is attributed to the inconsistency in the availability of jobs in such a saturated market. There is however the possibility of one getting picked up by big corporations that are able to offer a sustainable and reliable salary. In such an instance, then it may be taken as a full time job. The modelling industry is relatively intimidating and hard to break into; however with proper mental preparation, a determined mind- set, a commitment to artistry and good old fashion hard work a fruitful career is attainable.

Questions To Consider

Before an individual takes it upon themselves to venture into modelling or to take it as a career, there are questions that they must ponder upon. Figuring out the answers to these questions will help unravel the logistics of one's path and plan. These questions are packaged in these five forms: HOW, WHY, WHERE, WHAT and WHO. These questions are further elaborated and extended in the chapters to follow.

Why

Have you ever sat down and asked yourself why you want to be a model? Why you think you can make it in the modelling industry? Why you think you have the talent for modelling? The answers to these questions are innate and depend on one's own perspective, background and motive as an individual.

Some people model because they have passion for it, some model because of the money that they could get, while others model because they think they have the attributes of being a model. The chancers do it as way of experimenting and as a way of self-expression and trying out new things. The dedicated ones; however, model because to them it's a career and a passion that they love. At times people have this conclusion that models have what we call, beauty without brains "but remember, there is no work that requires training that does not involve applying intelligence and brain power. Not all models are graduates but not all models who graduated have natural talent or a special gift.

A person who is not professionally trained can supersede a master's degree holder in terms of success; all it takes is resilience and a fighting spirit. There is however need for a gift to be nurtured so that it can improve, be better and shine more. So in essence, because modelling is so energy intensive, people who choose to model should do so because they love it and because it is their passion.

When

When was the passion for modelling ignited? When is the proper time for one to model? When should one do events that deal with modelling?

Well the truth is, there can never be a perfect time, unless one creates it. Many people believe to model is getting on stage and wearing high heels or just walking through the runway. Modelling has rules and themes, you don't just model because you 'feel' you have what it takes, you must in fact have actual talent. Modelling is like any other dream, to live it you have to imagine it and to achieve it you have to work even harder. Through all this, timing is crucial. A model can show their skills during a fashion show, during runway practice and when in training to demonstrate their skills. Models are subject to a lot of scrutiny, so models need to put themselves out there when they are in their best shape of their life, to avoid unnecessary criticism. In order to keep up with the pressures they must be in the best physical, mental and spiritual health.

Most agencies consider skills over looks and without skills you can't make it in the modelling industry. So models should only put themselves out there when they are confident about their skills and abilities, and when they know that they fit the right requirements and can fit the criterion that is expected of them.

What

What does being a model entail? What is one's inspiration to model? What is one's fall back plan after modelling?

Being a model takes more than just pure belief in one's talent. A signed model contract is what officially makes one a model. While passion and love for the craft is a beautiful thing, there should be skill and capacity to match that passion. Having the right requirements is essential, some of those include: height, waist size, the potential to walk in heels or pose, and the knack to show clothes off with flare. The above mentioned, and a whole lot more are the basic qualifiers that one needs, to become a model. There is however the possibilities of possessing the right attributes of being a model and still not have the skills to execute it. In situations like this practice would be the first aspect that one should start with before anything else. Having these attributes is affirmation that one is in the right direction and that can take the necessary steps towards their dream of modelling.

Who

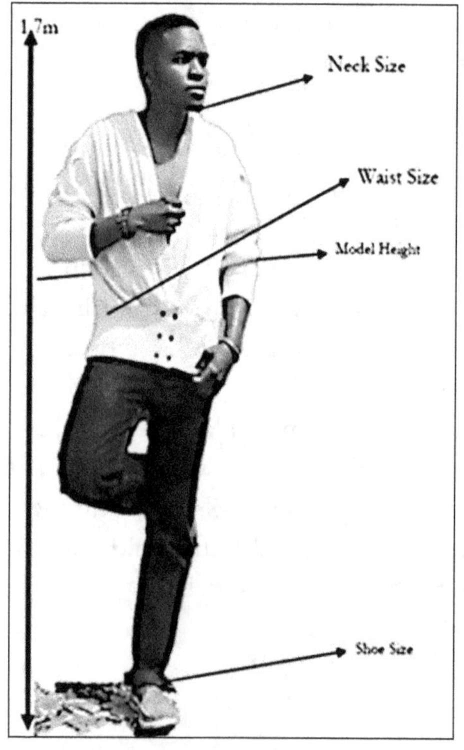

Who should model? Who decides whether one is a model or not? Who do deems one to be fit for modelling?

Anyone can model but not all people become models. The reason for this norm is that there are certain attributes and steps that one has to fulfil first. Many people think being a model is all about wearing beautiful clothes and shoes and getting on stage, or taking photos but there's much more to modelling one can ever imagine.

A model is someone who differs with the rest of the people in the sense of fashion, their walk and their talk. Models are considered to have a unique way of doing things and making things. Auditions are held by agencies in order to help unearth and reveal the talent that is undiscovered.

Most agencies consider the following requirements: models height, legal age, shoe size, burst size, neck size and weight. For other agencies and fashion designers that standard may vary due to choice and preference.

Those measurements and requirements should be done every after month or two month because of growth and change in body size to be certain and sure about one's measurements.

One can't use measurements from a year ago because they might not match reality now thus giving a false impression that could lead to disqualification. Here is a review of some of the requirements that were mentioned previously:

Types of Modelling

There are different types of modelling of as we have already stated, some of which include; Commercial modelling, Runway modelling, catalogue modelling, photo-shoot modelling, editorial modelling and fit modelling. These are only a few of the most common.

Photo-shoot modelling

This is when a model focuses more on taking photos that can be used in advertisements, billboards, flyers, magazine covers or magazine page features and posters. Photo-shoot modelling deals with taking pictures mostly focused on themes and certain type of posing.

A model should know how to best adapt to the set in order to portray the photographer's vision. Most models prefer taking photos on photo-shoots in order to make a z-card which they can use when networking.

Commercial modelling

Commercial modelling is another type that advertises products and services. A model may be asked to represent a company's product for promotional purposes. In most of the cases you may find that companies have new products that they want to advertise to people and in order to reach those people they need models to be their spokesperson.

Models who do commercial modelling may be hired and paid on a weekly basis or paid in hours depending on what the contract between them and the company that hired them stipulates.

Commercial Modelling can also be on a print media basis and be used to advertise products in their different ranges.

Fit modelling

Fit modelling can be done by any model of any body size; it is up to the agents or the organizer's of events to reveal the specifics on the type of model sizes that they require. Fit models mostly wear designer clothes which are created looking at what they want to show case and the clientele that they cater for. Models that have what is considered a perfect body size for a casting will then go to audition for those designers and agencies. Models that do fit modelling can be chosen looking at the size requirements, shoe size, height, and weight.

Runway modelling

This type of modelling occurs during fashion shows. During these shows models wear some designer clothes; they do an elevated catwalk on stage or any type of walk which will be determined by the theme, the type of the fashion show or the set that the organizers have planned to showcase.

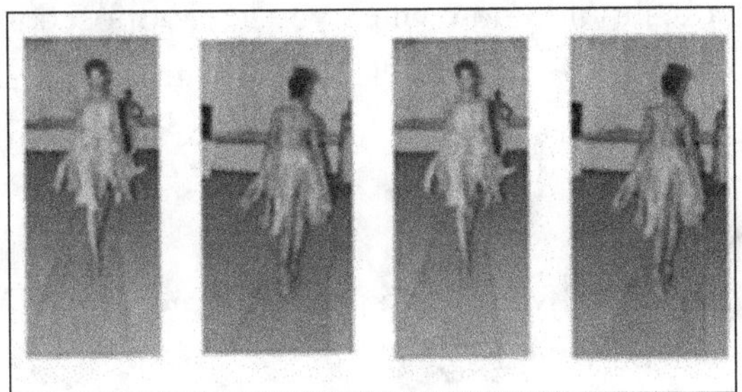

-Sample of a Runway Model.

Editorial modelling

Editorial modelling deals mostly with print media. This includes outlets such magazines, books and newspapers.

Catalogue modelling

This is a print modelling done to show case a company's clothing or products in their publication.

Questions On Types Of Modelling

Photo-shoot Modelling

What is the theme of the photo-shoot? Where is the time and venue of the photo-shoot and will you be sponsored with clothes or you will be bringing your own? Will you be doing your own makeup and hair? How much will you be your remuneration? Is there a contract that will be signed which deals with the terms and payment agreement?

Commercial modelling

The question is what are you advertising? You need to know your product to avoid having fall backs when customers ask you questions at your stall. You should know when you are supposed to advertise it, why you are supposed to advertise it, who you are advertising it to, how you are going to advertise it and where you are advertising it?

Fit Modelling

When and how will you be doing the fit modelling? Will there be special guests will be attending?

What are you branding?

Are you being sponsored to advertise as a fit model or they will the employer cover the costs?

Runway Modelling

Ask the place, time and dates of the event. What the event is all about?

What type of stage will be used?

The type of designs you will be wearing and if there will be a pre-show rehearsal before the event?

Editorial Modelling

What the theme of the shoot?

What are the time and the venue for the event?

Will the event organizers cover your costs or will you have to fund yourself?

What are the payment terms?

Catalogue Modelling

Enquire about compensation terms, times, dates and venue of the event.

What To Know As A Model

Walk

The way one walks should express on its own that you are a model. The walk should be distinctive, should show extreme poise and confidence. People need not enquire; it must be apparent from one's stance that they are self-assured and know exactly what they are doing.

Models should always consider speed when walking because speed is supposed to synchronize with the background music in a runway. As well, they should find the right pace because the audience needs to get a good view of the clothes. Speed is also a factor when changing in to different looks behind the scenes. Models need to be able to keep time so that they don't miss their turn or leave their audience waiting.

Always make sure you keep the focus on the target and the destination when walking the runway. Avoid looking down when walking or crossing your legs. Always maintain eye contact with where you are headed and make a clear way before walking ahead. Walking and looking down can end in disaster, i.e. on one colliding into things because they are unaware or maybe tripping down the other models that are in the runway.

Walking also controls one's head, body gesture and the way they move their hands. Avoid over swinging your hands when walking and also avoid folding your hands when walking. Maintain a set of balance through your feet and walk in a straight line to avoid going out of stage. Do not let nervousness make you lose control while on stage.

Talk

Character defines your attitude, and attitude determines how personable people find one to be. There is no one who would like to work with a model that is rude or does not take correction or guidance.

At times becoming someone you never thought you could be (attaining fame) changes people and they tend to forget who they are, where they used to be and what their aim was from the onset.

The best type of models are those who stand up to represent their community and for the betterment of not just their lives but the lives of everyone else.

They do campaigns for charity, they act as role models and they use their status in the society to inspire and cause change. They are humble, patient and polite people who are willing to listen and take advices.

Branding

As a model it's very important, that one takes everything that has to do with their job seriously and always maintain a high degree of professionalism. Always dress to impress and walk to invest. You will never know who is at the event you have been chosen to model at?

People who invest in talent want to see it at its best. So it's important to make sure one brands themselves, their name and the company or the event that they are presenting at as the best of their ability. In such social and business settings, (fashions shows/events) people take note of what they see and the impression that one leaves behind is crucial.

A model also has to be aware of the fact that branding does not come cheap. In order to earn they must spend. There is need for one to invest in oneself, in

order to maintain a high quality standard in order to attract the right people to one's brand.

As a model who represents a company one should always make sure they strike balance between themselves and the company because if anything defaming should happen there's a strong likelihood that one will drag the company down with them.

Fashion sense

When it comes to fashion it is important to have style that defines and not one that defiles. One's fashion sense as a model should make people take notice but in a classy manner. Models are very unique and creative beings when it comes to fashion and they love to trend but that should not be at the expense of dignity.

Models are mostly defined by what they wear and their peculiar look. So their outfits have to be properly thought out and coordinated so that they can cause an impact and create trends e.g. a statement necklace seen on a model can trend and eventually sell out in stores.

Photography

Always have eye contact with the camera when taking photos or even when posing in a different direction one can make sure that they still use their hands and legs to maintain a unique balance. Don't just take ordinary photos, make a mark by taking exquisite photos that will make people stand up and take notice of your talent.

Facial expressions

Always make sure you match your facial expressions with what the theme is. Facial expressions should be more relaxed and loosened up. Models faces are their money makers and they must be able to shift through different facial expressions to show different moods that are synonymous to the theme of a shoot e.g. Drama/comedy or sad/happy.

Nails

Nails carry the highest sense of hygiene. So make sure that your nails are always clean and blend well if you find the urge to use nail polish.

Hair

A models hair defines their outfit even more. Without the perfect hair style there's no cohesiveness in the look. There are so many hairstyles that a model can use. Keep hair in its natural colour unless requested otherwise.

Exercises

A model should keep fit and make sure they get enough exercises. Models wear heels most of the time, so exercise is required to help with stamina and balance, as well as maintaining a healthy weight. Pilates, aerobics and some jogging are some of the techniques that one can employ to maintain a healthy lifestyle.

What A Model Should Have

Every model must possess these two essential items, a portfolio and a z-card. A model portfolio is a compilation of pictures and videos of previous work done by a model. It shows the models? credentials i.e. Height, waist, age, contacts, E-mail, shoe size, weight, eye colour and any other information that may be included by the model or the fashion designer. A z-card on the other hand is a small card that has a model's face portrait and full body shot.

It is used when networking. Basically a portrait is a curriculum vitae and a z-card is practically a business card. A model should also have a daily planner that he/she keeps, that shows their schedule for events and jobs.

The photographer during a photo-shoot of the portfolio process gives a model the location, tells the model what theme they will cover and takes the photos. The duty of the stylist in this case is to take the model's measurements that is, waist size, height and all the others. After all is said done about twenty different photos are compiled. Those photos represent different themes of clothes and different locations if possible. A portfolio is the model in a nutshell; it speaks on behalf of them if they submit it at auditions or agencies.

A model should also have a strong sense of self. They should be aware of their own innate abilities and their strength and weaknesses so that they can best explore their opportunities. They need to know what best speaks to their personality and what speaks to them as a person. It is much easier and believable to the consumer if one endorses a product that is of personal repute to them.

Types Of Posing

There are three types of posing of which are the: up- straight posing, the middle posing and the ground pose.

The up-straight posing

Posing done standing, referred to as posing while up- straight. There are ways in which a person can pose while standing of which are: The run-away posing, overlapping in a group posing, neck twist pose, walk away posing or the reach out posing. Any pose done standing is an up-straight pose but which doesn't include bending a knee or being on the ground. Here is a sample we have provided below:

The Middle Posing

This is posing done in the middle field level. A knee or knees have to be blended. Middle posing can have poses such as hip hop posing, dance posing, the feel out posing, touch of reflections posing and many others. Sample is provided below:

The middle pose

The Ground Posing

This is posing done at the ground level. Such poses include: Crossed leg posing, neck bend posing and any other posing that may be included as a ground posing.

The ground posing can include such posing as: The gym posing, the leg posing, the lay back posing and any other ground posing.

The Model

Define Your Line Of Modelling

There may be auditions held by an agency and there may be fashion show auditions or a pageant being held. The question is have you defined your line of modelling, is that's the right agency to join and are these auditions in line with the path that you want to take as a model? Or are you just joining auditions because you feel the urge to be part of something?

A lot of models find themselves choosing the wrong routes because of wrong planning. Without proper planning there is no clear cut stance, so it's very important that a person locate their sense of path and what they want before they could join or decide to go for auditions. It's always good to do a background check on an agency and know them first before you can go for auditions. A lot of models end up dropping out of agencies because of misunderstandings that could have been avoided or even solved by a proper back story on both parties. It's imperative to know a prospective employee's aims, vision, mission or any ideologies that they adhere to beforehand to avoid being let down.

Another issue when dealing with an upcoming artist is that after a two months or three months training process they end up feeling bigger than the models that have been in the industry for years prior. Models should learn to keep calm and keep training. Success is an everyday training session not a one, two or even three day thing.

Define Your Niche

Learn to define your way of doing things, a way that is unique to you as an individual. There are many models but only a few of them actually stand out or become iconic. It's very important that one knows if they intend to be a trend follower or a trend setter.

Always make sure you define the type of legacy you want to leave behind. Whatever one wants to be known for or associated with must come out as part of the trend they set. For example, if its shoes you want to focus on make sure you love the cut, the fit, the colours and anything else that has to do with it.

As A Signed Model In An Agency

When you have been taken up by an agency always make sure that you sign contracts of agreements and that you know extensively the activities that you will be paid for and when you will be getting your remuneration. It's always very important to know beforehand what you will be facing and what you will be dealing with. You can invest to gain but make sure you don't invest to loose. A lot of models are left jilted with just pictures when photographers advertise themselves and they get the exposure.

While they get booked models just get seen. Make sure that every photo-shoot you do is also of benefit to you and that you are not just being exploited. There are however, times when you will need to work for free just to get exposure and to build up your skills as a model. So you should have saved certain money that can help you invest in yourself. Don't chase after money but chase after perfection and money will follow.

Signing A Model Contract

Always make sure to go through contracts and process them before you agree. There's no problem with refusing to sign a contract if you don't agree with the terms and conditions which have been set. But never sign because you are led by passion. Sign because you agree with what is put on the table.

A sample of a contract

AFRICAN *PORTFOLIO MODELS*

"Making memories, keeping memories"

Fill in the spaces provided and submit

I____ here in after referred to be signed by:_____________________________________
_ agree to be signed as a model in the field of modelling/training/ volunteer/for a fashion show under a period of_________________
_________________________ paid/not paid/paying them for service they providing me. 'Contract Period? will begin on day of arrival from the_
____ until ________________

_________________________________.

Agreement and general understanding

The Model, the Agency, and the Market will determine the success of any Model in events and payments for events are as per the agreement made between the two parties. Although the Market and Agency are not within our control, The Model and the Agency are. We must work together as the model and the Agency to promote the Model while the Model must diligently follow directions and instructions made concerning advertising, practices, promotions for the events and marketing. This spirit of partnership is essential for success and prosperity for both the agency and the Model.

By offering the Model a guaranteed income, the Agency, has taken on financial risk to agree on terms to pay models a certain fee regarding the type of shows, the events they will be involved in and activities that will promote them. Full cooperation will be needed to have a necessary feed liable to not this agreement and cooperation will cause the model to be terminated where possible and termination of contract if possible due to the director's decision.

This agency is the new onset of models with change and models with talents who will show case the finest onsets of runway, catalogue, editorial, fit, commercial models, photo-shoots and many more of which we will also collaborate with models due this time we will do some documentarians anything that occurs during events which will be well and not pleasing so that we can record and be able to create the change in models we want. We are also in the process of working on a magazine that will onset all talents but it is not only limited to modelling in Botswana.

Representation

Agency will exclusively represent Model in:

- Runway Modelling
- Catalogue Modelling
- Editorial Modelling
- Fit Modelling
- Commercial Modelling
- Photo-shoot Modelling

As a signed mode a payment of _________________________________ _________ will be issued to me per day/ in events/at fashion shows. I have experience/don't have experience in ___________________ _________________ and I have been involved in events/modelling agencies and designers like _________________________________

I as ___________________________________ also have talents in field of.

Payment Method

The models will be paid under various terms. Agency estimates that clients will be paid only after the events have commenced within 2-3 days as we will be processing funds and payment will be in the form of cash and a signed signature of the model will be required as proof of agreement to the terms.

Fill In The Details:

Models will be considered to fill in the following blanks and should be fully researched if possible:

Model Information

Name:..................... Date of birth:.....................

Contacts:................. Nationality:........................

Height: ....Weight:..............................

Eye colour:............ Waist:...............................

Shoe size:.............. Id number:...........................

Next of kin name & contacts:...............................

Place of birth: _______________________________________

Education Background: __________________________________

Residential and Place: _________________________________

The signed/voluntarily agree to the conditions set forth above. The agency has explained the contents of this Contract to the Model.

Signature of the model: ________________________________

___ Date: ________ Signature of the director: ___________

____

Date received: ____

This is some of the information that you may find in a model contract.

Agency Schedules

It's very important for an agency or a model to have a calendar that guides them on what activities will be happening during the course of their time with the agency or the course of the year while they are signed in models. Here's a sample of an agency calendar and some activities that a calendar created by an agency may provide.

Calender Of Events

Month	Name of event
January-february	Street reign
March	Boot camp
April-may	The word
June-july	Vintage fashion
August-september	Fashion brand
October	Folio photoshoot
November-december	Fashion forward

Meetings: Meetings will be held one day a week and on Saturdays of which the models are to agree a certain date that best suits them as per the agreement. Only termination of a contract will be done on December 28 and renewed next year if liable to do so.

The Agency

The Agency will provide the following for models, it will be of benefit to them especially helping them market, advertise and expose their talents.

VIDEO- TV PROGRAMME VIDEOS

-MODEL DOCUMENTARY VIDEO ON STAGE AND ABOUT THE MODEL

-Promotional works for books and videos for companies.

-T-shirt label for the models

-Clothing line label

STREET REGIN

-FASHION SHOWS

-PHOTOSHOOTS

Advertising The Models:

Television, radio, newspapers, business cards, fashion blogs, fashion shows.

- **How we will be raising funds**

Family fun day, photo-shoots, fashion shows

- **What we will be giving to the models**

Saloon treatments, gym lessons, shoes, English lessons, posters to advertise, clothes, walking lessons, tv program to help them get exposure, portfolio, z-card, make-up lessons.

Payment will be 1500-00 per a show and the company will be liable to the model and the model is requested to ask for payment five days after the event. Models also have to agree for promotional works and other things which we will recommend. Their photos and videos will be used to help in the form of marketing. Therefore models will only be remunerated for shows that are on the calendar and if possible food will be provided at events and at photo- shoots.

Don't Just Be A Model

Many people aspire to be models, because of a number of reasons, some want to just try it out, some do it for the money, and some do it because they have passion for it.

The modelling industry has a lot of young up and coming who are trying to break into it. A lot of them face rejection and fall on hard times because the industry is so competitive. But as previously mentioned there is more to the art and there is a lot that one needs to be in the know of.

Below are some of the well-known fundamentals that one can adhere to increase their chance of survival;

- Always eat healthy foods. Veggies, fruits, whole grains, healthy fats, and lean proteins should make up the basics of your diet. But sugars, starches, and unhealthy fats should be avoided as much as possible.

- Always drink a lot of water. Avoid taking sodas and minimize your alcohol intake.

- As a model have certain requirements that match to your style and how you want to look. There are many models with different looks, but make sure you have your own unique set of standards as a model. Something that will give you an edge or help you trend or be remembered in events and photo-shoots.

- Before anything else make sure that you maintain your appearance. Take the proper grooming steps because a model's look is their brand and improper grooming or lack thereof may diminish one's appeal to sell products.

Modelling Tips

Know more about the modelling industry; learn as much as you can. Visit agencies if possible, talk to experienced models, read fashion blogs, attend fashion shows or read modelling magazines and get know more about the industry you are faced with from the country of your origin.

Find role models that you aspire to be like. Doing this will help you improve your skills because you can use them as an example and for inspiration. Do your research as well and consider the type of agencies you want to be involved with or what you want to do as a model. Have standards and an intact moral code, and make sure you don't lose sight of them as time goes along.

Preparation is key, one must have a well thought out blue print of how they intend to progress in the industry. One must even be prepared to even go as far as investing in their own talent before they get the proper management to represent them. Overall is important to be fully prepared and be ready for both the triumphs and the challenges, and devise the best way to handle them. Striking a balance between the two and proper managing of both will help one to maintain longevity in the industry.

Fashion And Makeup

Going for a Casting

There are a couple of things that all models should invest in, to prepare for their modelling career. First of all, a basic outfit to wear when you go for castings or are being called to an agency for digitals.

If they are unsure about what to wear, black is always a safe option. A tank top/t-shirt and a pair of slim fitted jeans are the basics in such a scenario.

Shortlist for females:

The Do's

- A pair of slim fitted black jeans.
- A plain-coloured tank top or t-shirt.
- A pair of high heels (Ones with a simple design and a discreet colour).
- A pair of nude coloured underwear, both string and regular panties.
- Colourless lip balm.
- Hair should be slicked back and away from the face. (A simple pony tail is preferred)

The Don'ts

- Cocktail and Evening Dresses are not allowed: This includes any with shiny materials, chiffon, sparkles, lace, velvet etc.
- Tops and bottoms may not have large emblems, logos or numbers, stay logo free and model you.

- Outerwear is not acceptable.
- No athletic attire, cheerleading shorts, hot pants.
- Female models are allowed one accessory. No large or distracting earrings. Keep your accessories subtle.

Shortlist for the males

The Do's

- A pair of slim fitted black jeans.
- A plain-coloured t-shirt.
- A pair of plain coloured underwear, that fits properly.
- Hair should be simple, natural is always best

The Don'ts

- Keep your accessories subtle/neutral.
- No head gear or scarves allowed.

No carry-on accessories are allowed e.g. briefcases, umbrellas, cigars, cigarettes in holders, etc.

Being A Creative Outlet

The second stage of fashion modelling comes after a model has been picked up as a representative of a particular brand. During this stage the model and the designer enter into a synergetic partnership where both now represent each other. It becomes the designer's responsibility to blast the model into the spotlight as their brand ambassador and as well the duty of the model to use that spotlight to reach the target market that the designer was hoping to tap into.

For a certain period to be stipulated in the contract between the two, both agree that in that time frame they are a mirror of each other. For example if David appoints a model as an envoy for his creation, he/she is to wear his designs to all events where there is press, be it red carpet, radio or television interviews. This helps with the exposure of both parties and as well creates a buzz about the clothes. So the model literally becomes a walking advertisement, so he/she has to embody the essence of the brand that they are representing.

As of recent with social media having gain tremendous popularity, it has become a marketing hub and an easier way for brands to reach their consumers on a somewhat personal level. So in this instance the model would need to put up pictures of them wearing the clothes of the brand in order to create excitement around their collaboration.

This will help propel the customers? attraction to the clothing line that is in sale.

During this particular period the model will also walk in all the runways that are hosted by the designer as the head lining model. As the designer hits the different fashion shows in different cities the model walks in those to showcase the clothes to the audiences. This audience usually consists of the elite, celebrities, wealthy consumers, investors and competition in the form of other designers. So it is up to the model to not only sell the clothes to the consumer but to sell them to the potential investors and as well represent the designer in the face of rivalries. This means that the model must really be in tip top shape in terms of the body and their runway walk so that he/she makes the clothes look even more stunning.

So basically models, in terms of fashion must keep a clean, modest and natural look. The reason for this industry standard of simplicity is because for the most time models are canvases and the designers are the artists and their paint is the clothes that they design. This plainness allows for their elegance and beauty to surface, without the distraction of loud colours, excessive prints, heavy jewellery and accessories.

Make Up For The Model

Makeup is at the core of the fashion industry. It is used to create different looks, enhance certain features on the intended person and basically add to the already existing natural beauty.

Auditioning models and makeup

Models who are hunting for jobs are required per the industry standard to adhere of minimalism. When it comes to auditions, they are expected to go bare faced because this gives the scouts an idea of what the model naturally looks like.

The no-makeup rule helps the clients to see the model's natural skin tone and really get an idea of their untainted natural features. That helps reveal the model's flaws and how difficult it will be to hide them, on the other side their best features are left untainted to be further developed and enhanced.

Makeup Tips For A Job

For the model who has already booked a job, makeup is just an accessory used to enhance beauty and create looks that are in line with what the job is about.

Below are some of the basic rules that makeup artists use to create looks for different instances.

Choose your makeup well

When buying a makeup kit, models need to make sure that they choose something that is known for its quality.

This way, they are assured that the product will achieve the kind of effect that they are looking for. Aside from that, it also ensures that they won't experience any kind of horrible side effects on their skin with its use.

Consider your skin

When applying makeup, they need to make certain considerations to be on the safe side. For one, if they are aware of pre-existing skin allergies to certain types of makeup, then they should be careful when selecting makeup products to apply on it. Aside from that, they should also consider their skin tone so that they can enhance their beauty with makeup, as opposed to covering it with too much or altering it by using the wrong shades or products.

Consider your unique facial features

When applying makeup, models should also consider their unique features. Take the example of eyes. The shape and size of one's eyes are put to a number of factors, genetics and ethnicity being one of them. Because of that, difference models need to keep in mind that there is certain makeup techniques used for women with deep set eyes as well as for those with regularly set eyes.

By considering their eyes, they would be more able to come up with a technique that can enhance the beauty of their eyes more. The same applies for all the other facial features, it is best that a model know those features and knows what angles to use to best show them off.

Taking care of your makeup

There are certain makeup items, which should not be exposed to open air for a long period of time. The reason for that is that, it can become brittle or reduced in terms of quality. Therefore, models need to make sure that they close their makeup kit once they are done with it. They should store it in a place that is not too cold or too hot. Keeping it in such a condition allows for there not to be any alterations to the microbiology of the makeup, such alterations could affect the function of the makeup.

Keeping your makeup brushes clean

In most cases, when one is in a rush, they might end up leaving the brush they used in an inappropriate place, (i.e. bathroom sink). Once that happens, it opens the door to possible bacteria and fungi infections. So models need to be aware of where they put their brushes, advisably in a clean dry makeup box so that it does not come in contact with anything that could be harmful to the skin. This helps with time preservation as well because if it is always in the same place, it can be found easily in times of need.

Makeup for sensitive skin

For models with sensitive skin, it may take them some time to choose the makeup that won't get their skin irritated. Having allergic reactions from makeup is not something that one wants to experience. To go around it though, models can always do a spot test prior to purchasing a product. This can be done by applying a small amount of the makeup to their skin.

Wait 24 hours and see if they have any allergic reactions, before making up their mind. Such knowledge is very valuable because a model can inform every makeup artist that works on them about their allergies. This helps avoid a horrific situation where they get a reaction that can disrupt the line-up of the show, or even worse have serious health implications on the model.

Applying makeup for men

There is nothing wrong with male models who apply makeup, especially if they only want to cover certain imperfections. To do this, they can actually make use of the very basic makeup items. For example, to cover spots on the face, they can use a concealer for that and choose one that is a shade lighter their skin.

Makeup hygiene

It is very important that models practice good makeup hygiene. As previously mentioned their face is their money maker and thus needs a stringent care routine. Some of the things that they need to take note of when it comes to this would be the proper storage of their makeup items, cleaning the brushes, sponges regularly and many more. By practicing good makeup hygiene, they can prolong the life of their makeup items, and avoid spending a lot of money to replace them or even worse going to the doctor due to it.

Infected makeup

If Models get infected with a sort of disease, which they suspect came from their makeup; they should not be ashamed of it. They should still visit their doctor as soon as possible. If they experience allergic reactions, then they should take antihistamine which is medication that helps to reduce inflammation and pain, or better yet call a medical practitioner, so that they can provide medication to ensue immediate relief.

Using the concealer

It is quite impossible that everybody can be born with perfect skin. For some people influences like genes and the effects puberty, come with a lot of changes to the skin. For models that unfortunately bear acne scars or pimples there is hope. They can make use of a concealer to hide blemishes, pimples, or any other imperfections.

Though it does not offer a permanent solution there are things that one can do, in order to prolong its effects. One of which is to apply a light dusting on your face with loose powder. By doing that, they would be ensuring that the effects of the concealer would last for the whole night. This is good news for models that happen to have skin issues that cannot be fixed and can only be managed.

Using a lip balm

Lip balm can be used by both male and female models, although some of the males hesitate using it, by thinking that it is unmanly. However, using a lip balm can actually help in hydrating their lips.

Therefore, when they use it in adequate amounts, it helps to prevent or take care of cracked lips. Models quite often have to do a lot of acting, especially in commercials and advertisements.

Basically models need to take proper care of their skin if they wish to remain relevant and attractive in the market. The modelling industry is very competitive, with younger models rolling in with every passing day.

In order to achieve longevity models must take pride in their look and follow proper grooming routines that best suit them.

General Skincare routines for models

Even though makeup has essential minerals that can be beneficial to good skincare, if not used right it can negatively affect one's skin. Excessive and improper use of makeup can lead to dry skin, acne breakouts, skin blemishes and wrinkles, all of which propel the aging process.

In the modelling industry beautiful skin is pretty much an essential. It provides a clean base for most makeup artists and makes a model much more of a viable option as opposed to when they need a lot of work to mask their flaws. Here are some the basic guidelines that will help models and aspiring models to maintain a fresh look.

Never sleep with your make up on

The number one rule to using make up is that one never keeps it on beyond its need. As already mentioned, excessive use of makeup has debilitating effects on the skin, so sleeping while having it on will prove harmful to the skin. This may increase chances of bad skin developing and so it is best that models remove it at the end of the day and sleep with a bare fresh face. This gives the skin a chance to breath and regenerate.

Eating clean

A clean diet is not just essential for keeping the body petite or for weight loss only. It is also very important for the maintenance of good skin. Food that is high in sugar and fat content promotes the possibility of skin break outs and excessively oily skin, so it is best that one avoid indulging in such. The best thing for a model is eat mostly greens, (spinach, kale, cabbage), lean protein (fish, chicken, lean red meat), organic carbohydrates (brown rice, bran flakes) and only health fats like the ones found in avocados. Such food is said to promote development of healthy skin and gives a natural glow to the skin.

Regular cleanses

Every once in a while the body needs to be reset. One of the best ways to do so it a going through a colon cleanse. Cleanses are not just beneficial to the body but also do wonders to the skin. During the cleanse a lot of harmful toxins are removed from the body and some of the benefits of those damaging toxins being removed is that the skin is left feeling renewed. It would greatly benefit models to regularly cleanse and rehabilitate their skin.

Always moisturize

Moisture is important when trying to maintain or create beautiful skin. A great moisturizer will slow down the aging process and bring a beautiful and youthful glow to the skin. Great moisturizers have minerals and oils infused in them, and those minerals have a revitalizing quality to them that helps bring life to the skin. So as part of their daily skin care routine models can adopt this rule to help keep them looking fresh.

Exfoliate regularly

Exfoliating regularly is quite vital in maintaining great skin texture and look. Because the skin is constantly renewing itself by growing new cells, there is need to remove the dead skin cells that are lost as part of life and growth happening. One of the ways to do this is by investing in a name brand exfoliator that one can use daily. This will help remove the dead skin cells and leave the model's skin feeling refreshed and energized.

Drink lots of water

One of the basic ways to keep skin looking refreshed is by keeping it well hydrated. While there are other way to keep well hydrated (i.e. eating food with a high liquid content) the most obvious is by drinking lots of water. The recommended daily intake is two liters. If models make it a habit to adhere to this way, it will help keep their skin young and radiant.

Regular Exercise

Regularly exercise is important when trying to maintain a healthy lifestyle. When exercising the body releases unneeded salts and water through sweat. This helps to promote good skin care because some harmful toxins are removed through sweat. The mobility during exercise also increases blood flow to the skin, and that blood flow helps to renew skin and keeps it healthy-looking.

Fashion In Modeling

(Themes)

Casual Wear

There are times when individuals do not necessarily feel like dressing up or wearing something too extravagant, this principle also applies to models. In those instances of desired simplicity is when casual wear becomes a necessity.

For women, casual wear consists of simple dresses, jeans, skirts, t-shirts, simple flats and sandals. For the men this look comprises of simple jeans, shorts, shirts, plain t-shirts and sandals or loafers. This is an easy, everyday look that can be pulled off by any shape or size, however the model must be aware of what colours and prints best suite their skin colour and stick to those.

Formal Wear

This look is a little cleaner, polished and appeals mostly to the models who want to maintain a certain level of gravity in terms of class and sophistication. This look is also considered standard in the business world, so it makes perfect sense that this would be the attire that models spot when they attend meetings that involve the business side of the industry.

An example of such is when they go to deal negotiations, or when they go for contract signing when a deal has been finalized. The basics for formal wear for females are a pencil skirt, plain blouse and a slick blazer, or a basic pants suit. The jewellery that accompanies the outfit must be kept at a simple and minimal level. For males a basic three-piece suit and tie, with matching belt and cufflinks where necessary.

This outfit is finished off with a pair of simple solid colour shoes that match the suit.

Swim Wear

Swim wear is an essential in the modelling world. The reason for this norm is because that part of the fashion is highly popular with consumers, especially during the hotter seasons. In some countries it is even a requirement that models bring swim wear to auditions and castings, and the reason for that request is just for easy assessment of the model body and how in or out of shape they are.

For both men and women, there are a number of options available that favour one's shape or that just happens to fit their preference.

For females they can choose between a one piece bathing suit and a bikini, while for males it's either they go for trunks, swim suits or a speedo. While they have right of choice, the expectations is that, models adhere to more subtle and clean colours.

Street Wear

As of recent, with the rise of fashion bloggers and v- loggers especially on social media, street fashion has grown tremendously. Street fashion for a model is all part of branding and growing one's fan base.

It is important because it keeps models closer to their fans; street wear clothes not only appeal to everyone but are in most cases affordable to everyone. This type of clothing is mostly unisex, and consists of such pieces as, sneakers, hoodies, tank tops, ripped denim, leather infused items, heavily printed t-shirts, fur and a whole lot of heavy jewellery. Street wear serves the purpose of humanizing and humbling models, because for the most part, because of their job they are viewed as super beings.

African Wear

Quite popular in west Africa, African print has made its way to the rest of Africa and is now appealing to even the American and the European markets. This print comes in many colourful, unique and intriguing prints and patterns.

This look has evolved to a level where it is now associated with class, sophistication and culture.

This look is now used as a tribute to Africa's Afrocentric nature and history. Models usually spot this look in runway shows as part of their runway walk, and in their personal lives as well just to show their pride in African tradition and African history.

This print can be made into pretty much anything, be it suits, dresses, skirts, jumpsuits, blouses, tops. All of which are very appealing to the eye.